Elijah McCoy: A Life of Invention

by Kate Foster
illustrated by Taylor Morrison

Table of Contents

Remarkable Inventions SERIES

The Real McCoy

The expression "the real McCoy" is famous. It means something is the real deal, not a second-rate fake. There are many ideas about how this expression came to be. Some people believe it started with a black inventor named Elijah McCoy, who was born over 150 years ago. Elijah created dozens of inventions, from the folding ironing board to machines that changed train travel forever. All of his inventions were known for their high level of quality, and people often asked to make sure they had received "the real McCoy" instead of a cheap imitation.

Behind Elijah's great success, however, is his struggle against **prejudice.** This is the story of how he overcame the odds to bring his dreams of invention to life.

Born Free

Elijah was born in 1843 in a small farming community in Colchester, Canada. His parents had recently escaped slavery in the United States by traveling north on the **Underground Railroad.** In Canada, their family was free, but prejudice hadn't disappeared when they crossed the border. In fact, one of the McCoys's neighbors told a reporter, "The prejudice is higher here in this place than in any part of Canada." Elijah's parents treasured their freedom, but they dreamed of one day returning home to the United States.

The Underground Railroad

It was illegal and dangerous to escape slavery in the American South. A secret network of people offered slaves safe places to hide on their journey to freedom. Even though it was above ground and many people escaped on foot, the network was known as the Underground Railroad.

The McCoys traveled north to Canada to escape slavery.

Elijah had never known anything different, and life on the farm suited him just fine. When he wasn't at school or chasing an escaped hog through his family's cornfields, he could be found taking apart machines and putting them back together again. Sometimes he was shy around people, but Elijah never met a machine he didn't want to get to know better.

As a boy, Elijah tinkered with all kinds of machines, like this hand water pump.

Following a Dream

Not only was Elijah hardworking and curious, he had a natural gift for understanding machines. Everyone knew it—his teachers, his parents, and his eleven brothers and sisters. Some boys wanted to become cowboys, or gold miners, or farmers like their dads, but not Elijah. He was a kid with a one-track mind, and that track was to become a **mechanical engineer.**

Unfortunately, few people in those days were willing to train a black engineer in North America. So Elijah's parents saved whatever money they could, and when he was fifteen, they sent him to Scotland to study engineering. For the next five years, he would do nothing but learn about machines. For Elijah, it was a dream come true.

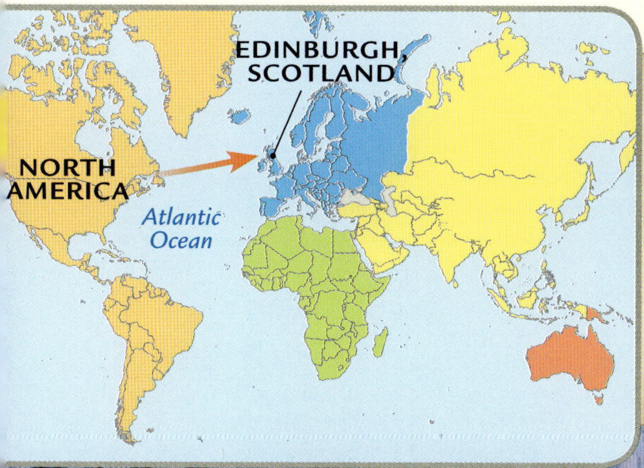

Elijah traveled over 3,500 miles (5,632 kilometers) before arriving in Edinburgh, Scotland, in 1859. His journey, by train and by ship, was long and uncomfortable. It lasted somewhere between two and five weeks.

The U.S. Civil War

While Elijah was in Scotland, a war that would end slavery was raging in the United States. Elijah's father, passionate about human rights and concerned about family members and friends still living in the South, signed up to fight for freedom. American President Abraham Lincoln ordered that all slaves be freed in 1863, but slavery and the war continued for another two years.

Railroad Days

Little is known about Elijah's years in Scotland, but he must have impressed his teachers. When he returned home five years later, a medal for his outstanding engineering work rested in his pocket, like a sign of the bright future that awaited him. His family had moved to Michigan in the United States, where the railroad was growing quickly. It seemed like the perfect place to get started on a new career as a mechanical engineer.

At that time, steam **locomotives** were 200 times more powerful than horses and could carry tons of cattle, people, coal, and lumber at what people then considered breakneck speed—about thirty miles (forty-eight kilometers) per hour. People wanted to be on the move and, in those days before cars, railroad lines couldn't be laid fast enough to meet the demand.

Elijah was full of hope when he went looking for work with the railroad, but he made a sad discovery. Even though slavery had ended, prejudice was still strong. Nobody believed that a young man with dark skin could be trained as a mechanical engineer. So Elijah took the only job he could get, as a fireman with the Michigan Central Railroad.

Dirty Work

The fireman's job was to shovel coal into a **firebox** to keep the **steam engine** running. It was dangerous, backbreaking work, but at least it gave Elijah time to think. He'd recently been married and started a family, and sometimes he thought about his wife and new baby. Often, because of the way his mind worked, Elijah thought about machines.

In those days, trains stopped frequently so that oilers, known as "grease monkeys," could scramble around to oil the engine parts. If they didn't, the engine could catch fire when parts rubbed together and became too hot or worn out. Grease monkeys were often orphans who worked for pennies a day, and their work could be as dangerous as that of a fireman. If a train started to move while a grease monkey was still oiling an engine, the result could be deadly. Elijah knew there must be a better, safer way to oil a machine.

Railroad Lingo

Life on the rails was filled with interesting expressions. The fireman was sometimes called an "ashcat" because he tended to be covered in soot from head to toe. Other times he was called a "bakehead" because his head was always near the firebox, heating up like a loaf of bread in an oven.

All Aboard!

In the last half of the nineteenth century, more black Americans worked for the railroad than for any other industry. Black workers served meals and carried luggage for train travelers, and they also performed many dangerous jobs, like that of the train fireman.

Elijah worked as a fireman on trains, shoveling coal into a firebox.

An Elegant Solution

After considering the oiling problem for a while, Elijah began to design an automatic oil cup that would supply just the right amount of oil to an engine. If it worked, long-distance trains, large ships, and factory machines would be more efficient and use less fuel. They would also be safer.

Night after night, Elijah worked alone in his workshop. After much trial and error, he finally felt he'd created a simple, elegant solution to the problem. Now it was time to tell the world about his invention. But some people refused to talk to him because he was black. They insulted his invention without even trying it.

Those who did try it, however, were impressed. His new idea meant that trains wouldn't have to stop every half hour for oiling—passengers could get where they were going faster. News of Elijah's important invention spread, and soon railroad workers everywhere were asking for the "real McCoy." Nothing else would do.

In about 1872, Elijah developed a lubricating oil cup that supplied oil to engines.

The Art of Invention

At last, Elijah was recognized as a mechanical engineer. Railroad executives wanted to hire him as an oiling expert, so he quit his job and started to travel around the country, telling people about his oil cup. It was a time of rapid change, not just in Elijah's life, but around the world.

Almost daily, it seemed, a brand new invention was making a sensation. How had people ever survived without the stapler, the zipper, the dishwasher, or the revolving door? The world was changing fast, and Elijah was right at the center of it all.

Era of Invention

A burst of invention took place beginning in the late nineteenth century. Here are just a few of the inventions Elijah saw during his lifetime:

1863	**bicycle**
1876	**telephone**
1881	**light bulb**
1888	**silent movie**
1892	**sneaker**
1893	**Ferris wheel**
1894	**breakfast cereal**
1903	**airplane**
1908	**affordable car**

Unstoppable

Once Elijah had begun to invent, there was no stopping him. In his spare time, he invented the folding ironing board, a lawn sprinkler in the shape of a turtle, a design for a tire, and another design for a rubber heel. Mainly, however, his inventions focused on finding better, safer ways to oil engines. Because Elijah was a perfectionist who made sure his products were top-quality, his oil cups and other inventions were always in high demand. Young people in his neighborhood began to look to him as an example. Perhaps if they worked as hard as Elijah, they might be successful one day, too.

Elijah showed some of his inventions to his daughter, Kitty, and his wife, Mary. This picture shows what his folding ironing board might have looked like.

Challenges

Though Elijah's inventions were made and sold all over the world, he continued to face **discrimination** at home in the United States. Many people wanted to buy the "real McCoy," but they didn't want to be reminded that the real McCoy was invented by a black engineer. Elijah was forced to sell his **patents**, the documents describing his ideas, to white-owned companies that could sell his oil cups and other devices. These companies made millions from Elijah's inventions.

Patent Power!

If inventors want to own their ideas, they have to apply for a patent. A patent is a document that says who came up with an idea first. Nobody else may copy a patented idea without the inventor's permission. In the years following slavery, patents were especially important to black Americans. Slaves weren't permitted to receive patents, and those who defended slavery said black people didn't have the talent or imagination to invent. Elijah, who patented over fifty inventions, proved just how wrong they were.

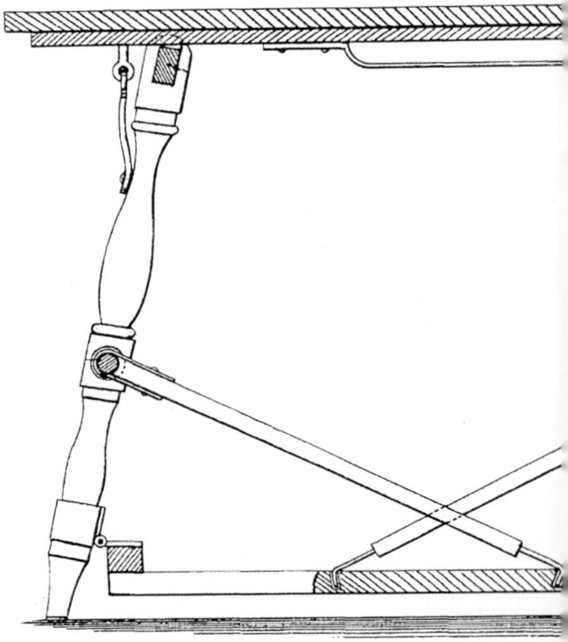

Though Elijah made a good living from selling his oil cup ideas and teaching others how to use the devices, he and other black American inventors often did not receive the respect they deserved. Sometimes when Elijah traveled around the country speaking about his inventions, he'd learn that one of his talks had been canceled at the last minute—when the organizers had realized he was black. At the grand fairs held to showcase the fabulous new inventions of the day, black Americans had to show their products in separate areas, apart from the white inventors.

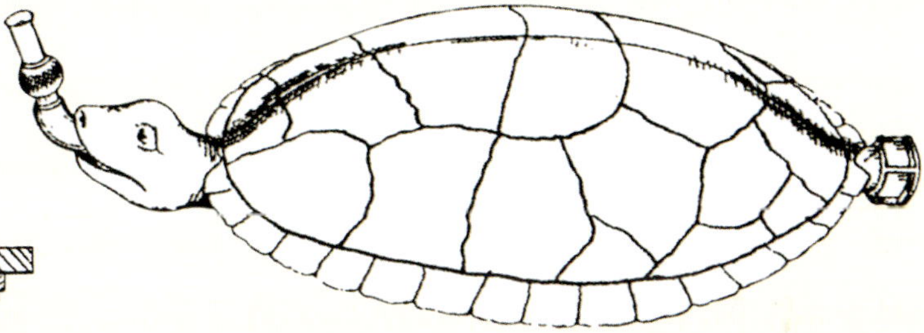

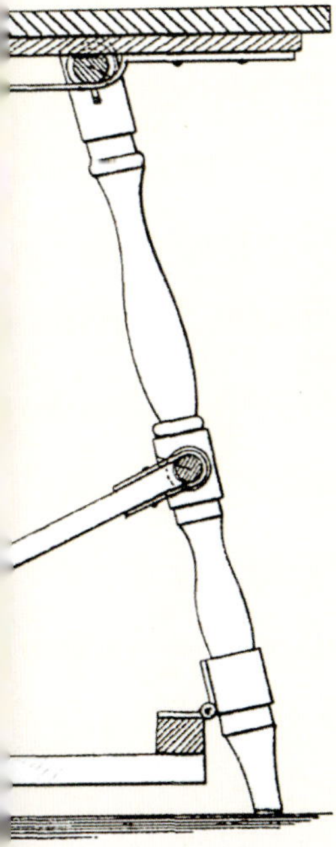

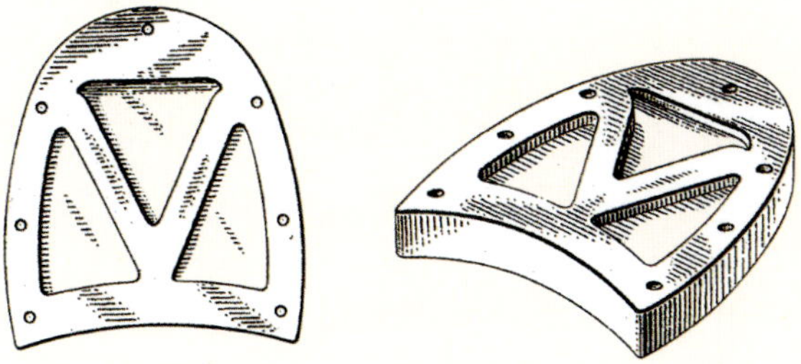

These drawings show three of Elijah's inventions, a folding ironing board, a lawn sprinkler that looked like a turtle, and a new heel design.

Despite these challenges, Elijah never slowed down for a second. Nothing, and nobody, could come between him and a mechanical problem. Each time he sold an invention, he'd put the money right back into coming up with an even better idea.

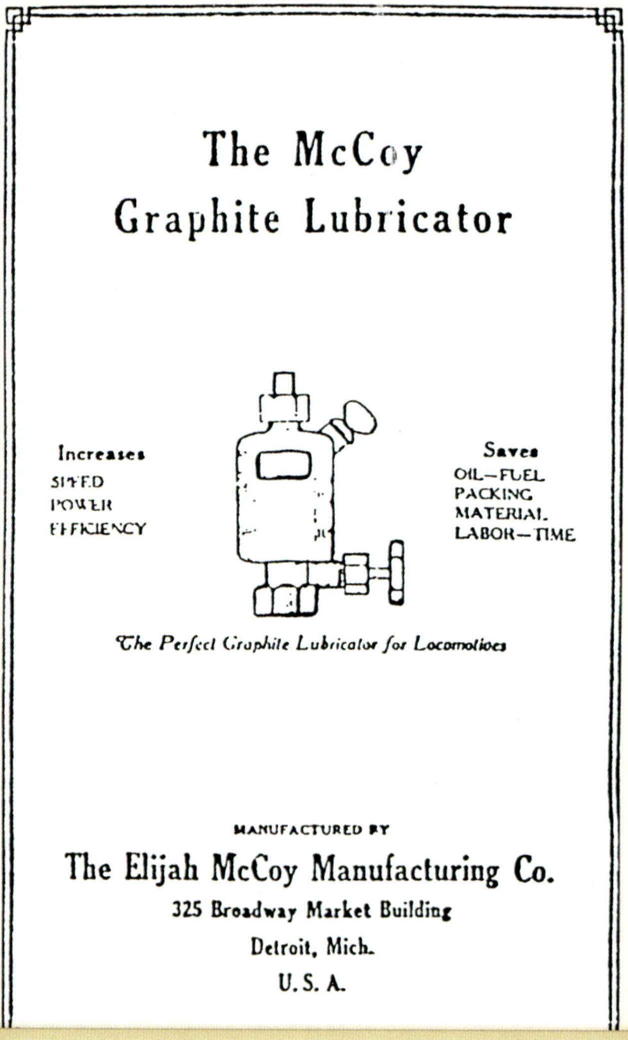

This is an advertisement for one of Elijah's inventions that helped trains run faster. One customer called it "the best thing in the world."

A Famous Name

Elijah's name had become so famous and respected by the early 1900s that a company called The Elijah McCoy Manufacturing Company was established to sell his latest invention—an oil cup that used graphite, the gray material used in pencils.

Elijah's invention was important because trains were going faster, and engines were getting too hot to use regular oil. He discovered that graphite mixed with oil kept engines running smoothly and allowed trains to run even faster. "Time is money!" the railroad executives liked to say, and Elijah's invention saved both.

Elijah didn't own the company that used his name and sold his invention, though. Customers knew the McCoy name meant that they were buying a quality product, but some people still didn't want to do business with a black engineer.

Perhaps if Elijah had been less curious about machines, he might have given up. But the same determination and love of invention that had led him to cross an ocean and face down discrimination again and again kept him inventing. In 1915, a writer described him as a man "upwards of seventy years of age, whose brain is still active in creating useful inventions for humanity."

Elijah kept working on new inventions as he got older.

Lost and Found

Now is the part of the story when this famous inventor, whose name is still recognized far and wide, should go down in the history books, remembered forever. Except that's not what happened.

Elijah died in 1929 at the age of eighty-six, penniless and nearly forgotten. He'd poured all his money into creating new inventions, his wife had died, and the arrival of the car had made his history-making improvements to steam engines seem unimportant. Elijah's story, it seemed, was lost.

Then, forty-five years later, writers and librarians began to ask questions. Who *was* the real McCoy anyway? They noticed that many stories of black Americans had been lost, and they wanted some answers.

They discovered that the people who remembered Elijah were the kids, now grown up, who'd once looked up to him as a role model. Besides his carefully drafted descriptions for inventions, some of Elijah's few words left today are the advice he gave to one young boy: "Stay in school. Be progressive. Work hard."

A Story to Remember

Though many people didn't believe that the son of escaped slaves could be a talented engineer, Elijah's imagination and love of machines proved stronger than the prejudice he faced. Today, people all over the world have benefited from his inventions.

In 2001, seventy-two years after his death, Elijah's genius was at last recognized when he was welcomed into the National Inventors Hall of Fame. Despite the obstacles he faced, Elijah showed that when it comes to invention, curiosity and hard work are an unbeatable combination.

Elijah gave advice to young men in his neighborhood.

Glossary

discrimination (dis-krih-muh-NAY-shun) n., when people are treated unfairly because they belong to a particular group or race

firebox (FYE-ur-boks) n., a closed area containing a fire, such as a furnace

locomotives (lo-kuh-MO-tivz) n., engines that pull train cars on the railroad

mechanical engineer (mih-KA-nih-kul en-juh-NEER) n., a person who designs and builds machines

patent (PA-tuhnt) n., an official document that gives an inventor ownership of an original idea

prejudice (PREH-juh-dis) n., dislike for a person, group, or race without a good reason

steam engine (STEEM EN-jun) n., an engine powered by steam

Underground Railroad (un-dur-GROUND RAYL-rode) n., a secret network of people who helped slaves escape from the American South before 1863